From Piggy Banks
To Prosperity

From Piggy Banks
to Prosperity

Teens and Money:

A Basic Money Guide

for the Teen and Young Adult

by J K Bowen

Contents

Introduction

I started this handbook as a convenient reference for my grandchildren, a guide to help them avoid poor money decisions and develop good money habits, but as I wrote and expanded, I came to the conclusion that others might benefit from this information as well. This is basic money handling for the teenager and young adult, but no matter your age, from 13 to 50, you will probably find useful information inside, broken down into easily absorbed topics. I'm not a certified financial planner or anything of the sort, and I am not offering advice on what you should or should not do with your money; after all, that is a personal choice. Instead I am presenting practical information in an easy to understand manner. I'm a father of five and a grandfather of ten. I've embarrassingly managed to survive a lifetime of self-inflicted financial wounds but I've learned from my mistakes and somehow managed to make a few wise choices along the way. I live a comfortable life in my retirement, and I hope that once you understand a few basics about money, you will be able to as well.

This book will not make you rich overnight. Accumulating any measure of wealth takes time and dedication, and you are the one who will have to make the decision to do so. You are also the one who will determine how much you need to accumulate and how much you want to accumulate. I can only help you get started. I begin with the simplest of topics and go from there. The Table of Contents will give you an idea of the progression we will take, and even if you think you have an understanding of the basics, I encourage you to read each chapter in the order presented. You might just find something of value.

Chapter 1 What is Money?

Money: What is it, where do we get it, and how is it used?

Money is the universal medium of exchange. Simply put, it is the accepted method to purchase an item, pay a bill or perform a variety of transactions. Money, or its recognized promissory substitutes, can appear in many forms, including cash, checks, credit cards, and debit cards.

If the universal medium of exchange was Pokemon Cards, Pez Dispensers, stuffed animals, music CDs, video games, or tennis shoes, nearly every one of us would know someone who is affluent due to their accumulated wealth of these items. But the universal medium of exchange is in fact money, so we'll just have to work with that.

So what should we do with money when we have it? How did we get it? Did we earn it? Did we borrow it? Should we save it or spend it? Well, why have money if we can't spend it, right? But should we spend it all or should we save at least a portion of it? We are going to find out and we'll begin with the very basics. This book is brief but full of valuable information.

We're not going to talk about coinage or the printing of money, or the Federal Reserve, or any of that stuff. We are talking about your own personal finances. Your money.

As a small child, you may have received token amounts of money from friends, relatives, the Tooth Fairy, or your parents for getting good grades in school or for successfully performing a simple task around the house, or for losing a tooth. Many children deposited this money into a Piggy Bank, a plastic or ceramic piglet that stood pompously in a place of honor atop your dresser or bookshelf, always smiling and always hungry to be fed more coins. Usually, the money stayed there until the day came when the child expressed a burning desire to purchase a game or a toy, whereupon the parent helped extract the money from the pig, counted it out, and determined if enough money had accumulated inside the piggy bank to make the purchase. This was usually a child's first savings account, and it was intended to instill a good savings habit in the child, a habit of saving toward a reachable goal. For most of us, this habit of saving eventually fell by the wayside as we grew into teenagers and developed a passion to spend money as quickly as we received it. For a teenager, there were so many things we deemed indispensable, and we needed a steady source of income to satisfy those needs. How did we get money? Teens just starting out usually obtained money in a couple of ways: an allowance, or a job.

What is an allowance? An allowance is usually a specific amount of money disbursed at certain intervals, for a specific purpose. Some teens get an allowance from their parents or other relative on a regular basis, and it is usually dependent on the teen doing something, most often for performing chores around the house such as cleaning, mowing, or carrying out the trash. The actual use of that money is often agreed upon beforehand and might be designated for such things as clothing, entertainment, school functions, etc. This is a personal matter between the giver and receiver, the parent and the teen. Some teens don't get any allowance, some get a lot. It all depends on the family's personal circumstances and their beliefs about money. Some get a large allowance for doing absolutely nothing, and I suspect they're the ones who grow up expecting the same arrangement with their employer, but that's just my opinion.

We can earn money by getting a job, and if you get an allowance for performing chores around the house, you are already working at a job. You are exchanging your labor for money. Eventually, you will probably want more money than your household chores can provide, and will seek out more jobs. Of course you should ask your parent's permission to find work outside your own home, but there are many jobs that are typically done by teenagers. A lot of them are jobs done for friends and neighbors, such as raking leaves, mowing grass, washing cars, or helping them build, paint or repair something. These occasional small jobs of different types are known as Odd Jobs. Baby-sitting and pet-sitting are popular teenage ways to earn money from neighbors and friends, and often turn into a regular gig that lasts for years.

As you grow wings and prove you are ready for more responsibilities, and as you age, you can often find work in commercial establishments such as restaurants, fast-food chains and grocery stores, small boutiques or nearby farms, doing whatever type of work that is available in your area. Once you find a job, remember this: that teenage job does not have to become your life's work unless you allow it to be, or you want it to be.

While you are looking for a job, keep in mind there are often state-imposed age restrictions on the type of work you are allowed to do or the number of hours you are allowed to work in a week, as well as parent-imposed limits. But if you want a job and your parents are supportive, you can find something to do to generate income. Usually, all you have to do is ask, beginning with neighbors or friends, asking about those odd jobs that need to be done. If you do good work for them, they can usually be used as a reference when you arrange to do your next job.

Eventually, when you decide to work more hours, you will probably be hired by a company that lets you work on a regular basis and pays you with a company check. Do not be surprised when your paycheck turns out to be less that you expected. This is the real world, and your employer will usually be required to deduct money from your paycheck and direct it elsewhere, to places like the federal government, your local government, state government, your retirement plan, your health insurance, a Health Savings Account, any legal attachments to your paycheck, and myriad other places that your money can go. The amount you have left after everybody gets their portion is known as your Take-home pay or your Net Income. This is the money you have left to work with.

It's tough for some teenagers who find that their income is necessary to help support their own household because Mom or Dad have hit a rough spot in their financial lives, but it happens. Sometimes you have to chip in on the family budget. Be grateful that you are able to help if necessary. For the most part though, a teen or young adult's income from outside sources is usually theirs to do with as they see fit. The parent should encourage them to save a little every time they get paid, before they spend it all. Otherwise, they do tend to spend it all. But how do we spend our money?

Chapter 2 Spending Cash

Cash: Indeed, at least in my opinion, cash is the best way to spend your money, and for this reason: If you have fifty dollars in your billfold, and that fifty is all you have, it is impossible to spend more than fifty dollars, right? You go out to eat with your friends and drop twenty dollars on a nice meal, then go to the mall to window shop. You discover that your favorite clothing store has an athletic jersey with your beloved team splashed across the front, and it's only thirty-five dollars. You look in your billfold to find that you have only thirty dollars left. A teenage dilemma. What can you do?

Well, you can come back another day with the correct amount of money, or you might just go home to think about it and eventually come to the conclusion that even though the jersey is nice, you aren't willing to part with your hard-earned money for that team jersey. And now if you check your billfold, you still have thirty dollars left.

Cash prevents you from spending more than you have, and a lack of cash prevents making a bad or frivolous spur-of-the-moment financial decision. If you eventually decide that you absolutely must have that jersey, you can always go back another day, maybe after your next payday and buy that jersey.

Cash forces you to recognize how much money you have left from the money you've earned.

I will concede there are a couple of instances where carrying or paying with cash might not be a good idea. First, if you are shopping in an undesirable neighborhood (and I will let you define undesirable), you might not want to be seen carrying more than a trivial amount of cash. The second is for a large-amount purchase, or something that might later need proof of purchase. If you paid cash and you later need to prove your purchase, you'll need that receipt. Do you know where it is? One way to prove your purchase is by paying with a check.

Chapter 3 The Checkbook

Using the checkbook is almost the same as spending cash, only you have to fill out all the blanks on the paper check properly. It takes some time to do, and your friends or the people in line behind you might let out a long sigh or give you an eyeroll while you fill the blanks, but don't cave in. It's your right to pay with whatever form of payment is acceptable to the seller. The absolute best thing about carrying a checkbook is that these things have a register in the back. A checkbook register is a place to record your transaction with the date, the amount, and what it's for... and is constructed so that with a simple subtraction, you will immediately know how much money you have left in your account, similar to peeking into your billfold. Plus, a cancelled check will be available from your bank should you ever need it. A cancelled check is the actual check you wrote, or more likely in today's times, a copy of the check you wrote, including endorsements (where the receiving party signed the back of the check). It makes for pretty good proof that you paid someone.

That is the good about a checking account. Of course, there is some bad to go along with the good. A checking account can cost you in a couple of ways. First, some banks will charge you a maintenance fee to handle your account. Usually, it is a few dollars a month and sometimes includes the expense of printing those checks with your name on them, but often not. Second, you will be penalized if you are not smart with your money. Keep in mind that if you write a check and the money is not in your checking account to cover the amount of the check, your account might be charged a fee – labeled NSF or Non-Sufficient Funds – for writing a bad check. And, in most cases, if that bad check is returned from the bank back to the merchant where you bought your merchandise, that merchant is also entitled to charge you a fee for writing them a bad check. In this case, you are out the added expenses of the bank's fee plus the merchant's fee. And it's all legal. (Overdraft Protection will be covered later) But this won't happen if you use that checkbook register and know how much money you have left to spend. By doing so you can avoid some of those pesky bank charges.

Also be aware that most banking institutions will not allow anyone younger than eighteen years old to open their own checking account. This means that a teenager will need a co-owner on the account, usually a parent or guardian. Once a co-owned account has been established, either party can write checks, make deposits or withdrawals, or totally drain that account. This demands the assumption of accountability and trust from both parties.

Grownups typically don't want to kick their kids to the curb, so they sometimes assume more responsibility than they realize whenever they sign or co-sign

13

documents for their children, and they often forget about it when the children reach the age of majority. My thoughts are that the parent and teenager should discuss the future ending of their account association before the account is ever established. This is true for many reasons, but one that immediately comes to mind is this: If the parent or the teen ever find themselves on the losing end of a lawsuit or other legal matter, any asset they hold, whether individually or jointly owned, may possibly be subject to attachment.

Remember this: you can always know how much money you have left to spend before you write that next check, simply by using the register in the back of your checkbook and keeping it up to date. A sample of a checkbook register can be found in the appendix at the back of this book, and as archaic as it may seem, it actually works.

Chapter 4 The Credit Card

The credit card is a plastic card with a unique number and a magnetic strip or a chip issued to you by a bank or other financial institution, and can be used to make purchases even if you currently have no money. Say what? You read that right. The institution predetermines how credit-worthy you are and how much credit they are willing to extend you. Usually it's more than you can comfortably afford. That's it. They send you a card and you can begin buying stuff immediately, as soon as you activate that card. Almost anything you want can be purchased with a credit card. You can buy from retail stores, grocery stores, restaurants, gas stations, game stores, and even make online purchases, and you can charge all the way up to your limit. The thing is, they will eventually want you to pay them back. With interest. How much interest will you have to pay? Let's take a quick look at money math, then we'll finish the credit card.

Don't panic. I'm not about to request that you solve any math problems in this book, but you should be able to do basic addition and subtraction. Otherwise, what's the use in trying to understand how money flows into and out of your hands or your bank account. Multiplication and division are useful tools as well, especially if you are borrowing or saving money. We're only going to address one formula in this book that you might think difficult. I won't take more than a minute of your time, and you won't have to work any problems with it, just be aware that it exists.

Is it this one?   **$E=mc^2$**

Look familiar? Everyone probably recognizes this formula. It's been taught in school for decades. It's on posters everywhere. But what does Einstein's Theory of Relativity have to do with managing your money?

Nothing. Absolutely nothing. You recognized it because it was pounded into your head at school, even though you never use it.

What about this one? **I=Prt**

Yes, this is the one that *should* have been pounded into your head. It may or may not look familiar. Like me, most people dismissed this as "just another math problem" when they were in school. That's unfortunate, because from the moment you open your first savings account or you sign your first loan papers, this formula is in play. It can either work *for* you if you're a saver or it can work *against* you if you are a borrower. This formula, I=Prt is the basic formula for computing interest. Interest = Principal x rate x time.

You don't have to work it, but when we talk about credit cards, savings accounts, or student loans, just know that this formula is constantly churning away in the background, usually in the lending institute's favor. We will talk about interest and interest rates in a moment, giving examples of how interest affects your money, but I promise you won't have to solve any math problems. I hope you're not bored yet, because we're just getting started, and these are things that you need to know.

That I=Prt formula we just looked at? That's a simplified version of the formula that lenders use to calculate how much you owe them for the use of their money. Our particular formula calculates interest once each year (when time=1), while their more refined formula calculates the interest on a daily basis. Yep, they work that interest formula on what you owe them 365 times a year. It seems that you end up paying interest on the interest, plus the original amount that you charged to the card. You have to be careful, because the maximum you are allowed to charge to the card is not the maximum that can accumulate on your account. That accumulated interest adds up quickly and can exceed your maximum limit. Of course, that's what the bank wants. That's where they get their money.

"So how much will I have to pay back each month?"

That depends on many factors. Usually, the minimum payment will be somewhere between 1% and 3% of the balance, or a fixed dollar amount such as $25 or $35, depending on your current balance. That's the absolute minimum you are required to pay to remain in good standing. "So that's all I have to do? Pay back a minimum amount, and I can buy anything I want?" Well yes you can, but trust me, **you do not want to pay only the minimum due,** and here's why: Paying only the minimum amount will trap you into paying forever. Repeat after me: For...ev...er.. The following is an example:

Let's assume the engine goes out on your car, and it costs $5,000 to have it replaced. Coincidentally, you have a brand new 11% credit card with a $5,000 max. Sounds like a match made in heaven, right? Well, maybe not. Before you swipe that card, let's look at the end result.

If the interest rate on your new card is 11% and you pay back a $150/month payment, you can get your engine replaced and be back on the road for only $150 a month! Yay!

Wait. For how long? Surely it will be paid off within a year, right?

Absolutely wrong. That engine might possibly be due for replacement again before you ever get the thing paid off, if you pay only $150 a month. Paying $150 will stretch those payments out, in this case for fifty-one months, according to an online calculator. Over four years! But be aware that as a new young credit card holder, you probably won't get a card for 11%. You might get an introductory rate of as low as 0%, but after the first year, your rate will skyrocket! Most likely, your new rate will be something like 25% or more. Paying a minimum amount, less than the minimum amount, missing a payment or paying late (there are charges

20

added for these), you could possibly find yourself paying on that $5,000 engine for over twenty years! Most likely, by then you will driving your third or fourth or fifth car and still paying on the engine for that first car. Don't think it can't happen to you. It happens to a lot of people a lot of the time. Do you want to be next?

So how do you avoid the credit card trap? A few things to keep in mind: If you have one, use your credit card sparingly. Pay more than the minimum required every month to keep that money-eating monster at bay. In fact, some credit card companies will forego the interest on your charges if you pay the entire balance in full each month. You might try to find another source of money such as a local bank or credit union to finance your engine, comparing interest rates of course. Or, if we had been putting some of our money away, saving it, we might have enough to pay for the engine, or at least part of it and not need to charge all of it to that credit card. This is one example that shows how saving some of your money might be a wise thing to do.

Since the Credit Card act was passed, you now must be age 21 to obtain your own credit card, or 18 with a co-signer (or sometimes with proof of a steady income). However, you can become an Authorized User of your parent's card, often as early as thirteen years of age, depending on your bank's policies. Like a joint checking account in one respect, this requires trust and responsibility from both the teen and the parent. If you are an authorized user on your parent's card, please show respect and restraint when you do use it.

Okay, that's the credit card. Now you know to beware. It can become a convenient friend or you can easily become trapped in a financial quagmire. How you use it is up to you.

A visually similar way to purchase items is up next, and in today's world, getting that Debit Card is like a rite of passage into adulthood, a trophy to show that you're all grown up.

Chapter 5 The Debit Card

The Debit Card: Swipe, swipe, swipe that card. Yes, we're talking about the debit card. It's easy and convenient, and we're tempted to swipe that card at every occasion. But there can be pitfalls, penalties and consequences. A teenager can usually get their own debit card as early as age eighteen, but can become an Authorized User of their parent's debit card at a much earlier age, often at age thirteen, depending on your bank. That doesn't mean that the parent is obligated to hand out debit cards to each of the children once they become teenagers, because as I mentioned, there can be pitfalls and consequences. Before a teen graduates to a debit card, they need to understand how it works. And it's pretty simple, actually. It works like an instantaneous check-writing tool and in fact the money comes directly out of your (or your parent's) checking account. Instead of painfully writing out a check in front of your impatient friends, you can be cool too, by just swiping that card. But be mindful, that money is subtracted from your account at the speed of light. So before a teen is entrusted with a debit card, they need to know how to balance a checkbook, or how to reconcile a balance sheet. (Reconcile: To compare one thing against another to ensure they agree.) And it's easy. It's fourth grade addition and subtraction. Let me repeat. **It's fourth grade math**. Forget trigonometry, algebra, geometry, calculus and all those other high-school headaches. This is fourth-grade math. All you have to do is write it down and subtract. Let me repeat myself once again: **All you have to do is write it down**… and just like peeking into your billfold or looking at your checkbook register, or breaking open your piggy bank, you will be able to see right then and there how much you have spent and how much you have left. It is so easy, yet so few do it. Write it down. It is also wise to check with the bank on a regular basis to ensure that your written-down balance agrees with the balance they show for your account. There's no need to call your bank after every purchase, and I can tell you that they will get tired of you in a hurry if you do that. But you can usually check online, or if you make regular deposits in person, they will give you a receipt for your deposit and most often, your current balance will appear on that receipt. Right then is the time to verify that your numbers and the bank's numbers agree; if not, you are standing right there, so ask the teller to explain the disagreement between your numbers. Most tellers will be happy to help you.

It's so effortless to swipe a card… swipe it here, swipe it there, and swipe it everywhere. Easy and convenient. Everybody does it. But what if we accidentally swipe once too often? What if we accidentally swipe *more* than once too often? If you keep a balance sheet, there's no reason to "accidentally" swipe that card when there's no money there. But life happens, and people do indeed swipe when there's no money left, and your friendly neighborhood bank has a solution for that… it's called Overdraft Protection. That will fix it! Or will it?

Overdraft protection sounds like a good idea, right? If we - for some reason - spend more than we have available, the bank will cover for us until we get more money. How's that for convenience? What a wonderful bank we have! They trust us to be responsible with money and cover for us when we're not! How great is that? The Overdraft Protection can automatically suck money from your *savings* account if that account is linked to your checking account, or if not, the bank automatically "loans" you the money from your line of credit to cover the purchase. So what's the downside?

Well, unfortunately, there's a charge for using your Overdraft protection. Yes, there are fees incurred each time that overdraft protection is used, typically $25 to $35, and if you're not careful, those fees can ruin you.

To illustrate how this convenience can quietly destroy you, I will provide an example that I am very familiar with.

A middle-aged woman confesses to my wife and I that she is broke and doesn't know why she is broke. Can we help her? Her once-a-month paycheck is direct-deposited into her bank account at the end of each month, and is usually around $3,000. She was sure she hadn't spent her entire paycheck, but she had no money left. We had to prod her to produce her latest bank statement. One quick look at her statement showed us what she already knew and didn't want to accept... almost her entire paycheck, nearly three thousand dollars, had been used to pay overdraft fees for that month and fees held over from previous months! And lest you think that can't happen, I assure you that it can, it does, and it will. The problem? Swiping that card and *assuming* that there was enough readily available cash to cover each purchase. It wasn't the bank's fault, it was hers!

Had she, even once during that month, checked her statement or her balance, she would have known about - and been able to stop - that bleeding of hard-earned cash. But she never checked it. She apparently hadn't even checked it the previous month or the month before that. She was all about online banking and electronic payments and automatic withdrawals, and swiping that card for everything, because that was what her generation did. She made assumptions every month about her finances. It could have turned out okay if she had only monitored her money. But she didn't, and this story is far from over.

In fact, she had enough overdraft fees accumulated to eat up a large part of her next paycheck as well. Fees just waiting for her next paycheck to hit that account so the bank could grab more of her money before she ever saw a dime. And by the time her next paycheck arrived, there were even more fees because even though she stopped swiping that card, those automatic bank drafts (for utility bills, internet, phone bill, etc.) just kept on coming. The automatic bank drafts each triggered a NSF and associated fee, or an overdraft and its fee, and these companies can hit your account again and again, each time costing you a NSF fee or an overdraft fee. In case you haven't figured it out by now, any form of "protection" you have is designed to protect the bank, not the account holder. They're going to get their money. Thirty-five bucks a pop for every overdraft. That $1.50 soda this lady bought on the way home from work earlier in the month cost her $36.50 ($1.50 + $35.00 overdraft fee). And again the next day, $36.50 for a soda. She never knew she was paying that much due to her "protection". And even more ironic is the fact that, at least at this particular bank, she could not put a stop to her overdraft protection until the bank had been reimbursed for all the accumulated overdrafts and monies they had paid on her behalf. So here she is, behind about six thousand dollars, and still has to come up with even more money before she can put a halt to the monster that is eating her money. What a mess. And it's all legal. This is an extreme example, but it's a true example. We never did find out what the initial "trigger" was to throw her account into overdraft protection because she didn't want us to see her prior month's statements, but her perpetual swiping - and never checking her account - was the root cause of her financial pain. These things happen, but do not need to happen. So before a teen starts swiping that card, make sure he or she promises to check that account balance often for any irregularities and can reconcile that account by using what? Fourth grade math.

Chapter 6 ETF

Since we mentioned automatic bank transfers, or Electronic Fund Transfer in the previous chapter, we will touch upon it here. Yes, you can have your regularly occurring bills set up to automatically be transferred from your checking account to a payee designated by you. These EFTs are designed to make sure your money gets to its destination at a certain time every month to avoid late charges from your phone company, utility company, or other destination.

The good part is, these keep you from incurring late charges from the payee, and I guess by now you can visualize the downside. Yep. If the money is not there when the transfer is set to occur, you get to pay your bank a NSF or an Overdraft charge, or you may get to pay a late fee to your utility company. So how can we be sure the money is there when it's time to transfer? Keep track of your deposits and purchases. Add, subtract, and write it down. Fourth grade math.

EFTs are also used if your employer pays you electronically. The money transfers from your employer's business account to your personal account without a paper check and without the intervention of a bank teller. If you are part of a Retirement Savings plan through your employer, such as a 401(k), chances are that the fund managers receive the deposits for your account in the same way.

Chapter 7 Money Between Friends

Lending and Borrowing between Friends: We have to put this somewhere. It might as well be here: Once you have earned some money, you are going to run into the friend who is "running short this week" and wants to borrow a few dollars until they get paid. Typically, these conversations take place at the local burger joint or the mall or the lunch line at school, and sometimes it feels benevolent to be able to loan money to a friend in need. But beware.

Helping a friend might be a nice gesture the first time. But when the second time arrives, and the third and the fourth time, it should be obvious that your friend has a cash flow problem. Sometimes these loans work out and sometimes they don't, but eventually, once they have established their ability to pay you back, they will hit you up for a large amount. My experience has been, that's the last time you will see them. They will soon find a new friend who is willing to hand over money, and they will work that new friend until it's time to move on to another new "friend". Not everyone is like that, but these people do exist. Other times, they will hit you up for a large amount the first time, then disappear.

An example of my stupidity in loaning money to a friend: One of my supervisors met me in the parking lot at work one day and asked if he could borrow $500 until payday, to help him over a rough spot. Sure, no problem. I went to my credit union, which was only a few blocks away, withdrew $500 and handed it over to him. After all, this was the guy who assigned my jobs, signed off on my time sheets, all that and he was a friend, too. Before he had a chance to pay me back, another "emergency" came up and he asked for another $500 until his money problem cleared up. I loaned it to him. Another couple weeks went by and I had a medical issue that required surgery. I was out of work for over a month, and when I came back to work, he was gone. An internal investigation found that he had borrowed $500 here and $1,000 there from friends and coworkers at our work facility before the company found out and got rid of him. His estimated take was between $35,000 and $40,000 dollars, all from people who knew him and trusted him. So much for friends, huh? From what I've experienced, friends and family can be the worst when it comes to paying you back. Now you know.

And if you are the one who needs to borrow from a friend, do it once, make sure you pay them back, and never do it again. Instead, figure out why you had to borrow from them in the first place, then fix it.

Chapter 8 Interest

The time has come to take a closer look at our interest formula. For savers or investors, this formula reveals the interest that your money earns. The **Interest** (money you earn on your savings, or the money you pay to borrow from a bank) is equal to the **Principal** (the amount saved or borrowed) multiplied by the **rate** (interest rate as a decimal) multiplied by the **time** (length of time invested). Currently, interest rates on savings are very low and you won't see much return on your savings at a bank or Credit Union, but let's look at an example anyway.

Assume that you have $1,000 in a savings account earning 1% interest. The interest earned for one entire year, using the formula I=Prt is this:

I=$1,000 (**Principal**) x .01 (**rate**, expressed as a decimal) x 1 (**time** in years). I = $1,000 x .01 x 1, and when you solve for I, you end up with a total return on your $1,000 savings of $10 dollars. Your savings account now has $1,010 in it. This is assuming simple interest, compounded annually. That $10 is not much reward for having your money tied up an entire year. But it is what it is.

For comparison, let's borrow that same money. Let's look at a bank loan or a credit card with a 29.9% interest rate. The interest you will pay if you borrowed that same $1,000 is this:

I=Prt, so I=$1,000 (**Principal**) x .299 (**rate**, expressed as a decimal) x 1 (**time** in years). You will pay back your original $1,000 plus $299 interest. This is assuming your interest is simple interest and calculated annually, which it is not. Most lending institutions calculate your interest daily, which adds accumulated interest onto the amount owed. You will find yourself paying interest on the interest, as well as the principal. (In the example we just used, your actual payback will be closer to $350, for an Effective Interest Rate of around 35%). Effective Interest Rate is the final, total cost of paying back your loan, expressed as a percentage, and includes such things as interest, fees, document preparation, etc. And it's all legal.

Let's raise the stakes a little for a real eye-opener. If we increase our one thousand dollars we've saved to ten thousand dollars, we will earn a $100 bill for our year-long saving efforts. Meanwhile, if we borrow that same $10,000 the bank could earn $3,500 for their efforts.

You probably shouldn't be surprised to find out that the bank takes the money you lend them (your deposit) and pays you 1% for the use of your money, then turns around and lends that same money out to someone else, or even you, charging interest rates of 15%, 20%, or more. The bank makes their money on the difference. Now it really seems unfair, but at least it should be clear. Again, it is what it is, but as long as you are aware, you are better equipped to make a difference in your financial decisions.

We have covered the various methods used to spend our money such as cash, debit cards, credit cards, etc., and touched upon basic interest examples, but before we can begin spending money we'll need to have some of it. Let's go get some money.

Chapter 9 Jobs

Jobs, jobs, and more jobs. You want or need a job to earn money. There are plenty of choices for a teen starting out or a young adult seeking independence and they might depend on individual circumstances, your location, or any special talents that you have.

My first paying job was helping a friend of mine rake leaves in his neighbor's yard. The job paid 35 cents. I ended up doing most of the raking because my friend explained that he was the one who "got us this job". And when it was time to divide that 35 cents, my friend got eighteen cents and I only got seventeen cents, because as he pointed out, it was his rake. That's the last job we did together. Keep in mind, seventeen cents was a lot of money back then (1958) for an eight-year-old. Nowdays, that same job probably pays $50 or more.

One of my neighbors pays $60 to have her yard cut on a weekly basis, and it takes less than an hour to do the job. If you're already onto the math, the guy cutting her yard earns $240 a month for mowing this one yard. There's nothing wrong with yard work, and it might prove to be a good start for a teen. You can start with your own yard and go from there. I know a couple of people who started out mowing grass as a part-time side hustle (in their thirties and forties) to earn a few extra bucks, and soon quit their regular job to do lawn maintenance. Yes, the pay can be good, although it will be seasonal in many parts of the country. There are many other jobs, such as wait-staffing, window washing, carpet cleaning and janitorial work. Sure, maybe they're not your ideal jobs, but they don't require a large amount of specialized training, and I'm satisfied some of these people out-earn the doctors whose windows they wash or yards they mow, or carpets they clean.

I once asked a friend who owned a carpet-cleaning business to clean our carpets. He was running a $99 special for the first three rooms, which was what I wanted, yet he insisted on doing our entire house. I didn't know how I was going to pay him the extra money for the entire house, but when he finished and I asked what I owed, he began laughing. I didn't get the joke, but he finally told me what I owed: "twenty-four cents."

He continued, "The chemical I use comes in fifty-pound bags, and costs me about eight cents a cup. I used three cups cleaning your carpets. My van is paid for and my equipment is paid for. I used your hot water and your electricity. I'm out twenty-four cents. Do you want to pay me now, or do I need to send you a bill?" Friends...

Although today's cost for same chemical would be about $1.25 - $2.50 for 3 cups, the profit margin is still there. Sure, the lawn-maintenance guy and the carpet cleaner each have a sizeable investment in their equipment and they work hard, but the point is, you can't assume the income of a certain job by the type of work the person does or the clothes they wear or the money they spend. You just can't until you know more about the job or the people who do that job. Some people wearing suits and ties are struggling every day, and some wearing dirty dungarees have money to burn. You have to do what speaks to you and makes you money and teaches you responsibility. Right now it's just a job. And sometimes those jobs eventually turn out to be careers.

So what exactly is a career? A career is a job that becomes a lifetime occupation. At this point in your life, you needn't commit yourself to a single idea. Keep your eyes open and your options open to find a new career, and if you don't find your career, perhaps your career will find you. An example would be a person who is good with numbers and desires to become an accountant, but after nursing a sick animal back to health, decides to become a veterinarian assistant. Either choice might be a good fit for this person. Your choices might be numerous if you keep an open mind and listen to what speaks to you. However, since this book is about money, I would be remiss if I failed to mention that the career you select needs to pay well enough to support your life's aspirations.

Let's take a few minutes to look at some good careers, and we'll start off with careers that don't require a college education. Let me repeat: **These careers do not require a college education.**

Chapter 10 Skilled Trades

Skilled Trades: Electrician, Plumber, Machinist, Welder, Carpenter, HVAC Technician, Aircraft Mechanic and more, if you are a hands-on type who would rather be outside fixing something, building something, or even tearing something apart to see how it works, the highly-paid skilled trades might be a good fit for a full-time career. Opportunities can be had by several means, but you often have to ask. That uncle who is a machinist, for example. He can probably steer you in the right direction to get started. Or the neighbor who works wiring houses and commercial buildings. Ask. Want to be a Cable TV Technician? Certainly don't interrupt a technician while he's on a pole thirty feet up in the air, but if you see his truck parked at the local Dairy Dip, it will be easy to spot him inside. Same for a telephone technician. Either one is likely to have a tool belt strapped around his waist. Stop in and ask. Although the occasional person will tell you to get lost, for the most part they will be willing to tell you what the job entails and how to get started.

You can ask at your local Union Hall. Usually, there will be brochures or pamphlets inside about their trade, and often someone inside to talk to. Unions sometimes work with companies in what's called JATC or Joint Apprenticeship Training Committee, wherein a young person with some knowledge and a desire to learn might find themselves in an Apprenticeship Training program where you get paid to learn. Let's repeat that. **You get paid to learn**. Typically, starting pay is about 40 to 60% of journeyman pay, and the workday is spent learning through on-the-job training, actually working, and classroom work. Typical programs are four years, and you can expect to receive a pay raise every six months, assuming you are learning and performing the work and progressing as expected. Yours truly went through one of these programs, and I can highly recommend it. If this has appeal, search the web for JATC programs to find out more information about any opportunities near you. Pay and benefits are great. Of course, depending upon the trade, the more proficient you are in math and science, the better your chance of landing one of these prized apprenticeships. After all, the carpenter and welder often need to measure and cut angles precisely, the machinist works with thousandths of an inch, the HVAC Technician needs to understand pressure, airflow and temperature, etc. You don't have to be an expert to get started, just be aware that these basic school subjects – math and science - will figure into your acceptance, training and daily work. Oversight of Apprenticeship programs may be either Federal or Industrial depending on current needs, and sometimes which way political winds are blowing.

One final note about these skilled trade jobs: Most of the people in these professions can usually find work in any city or town in the country. Of course the pay is generally better when you work in a large city or in an industrial-type environment, but even the smallest of towns will have need for an electrician, a plumber, a heating-and-air person, a welder, etc., so if things don't work out for you in one geographic location, you can usually find work in another area, or start your own business wherever you like.

Chapter 11 Military

Military: Another place where you can earn while you learn is the Military. It doesn't pay much to start, but when you figure that your food, clothing, housing, medical, etc. is furnished, maybe the pay isn't so bad after all. Plus, they teach you a skill that is often useful outside the military. Throw in a hard-to-beat retirement plan and the aforementioned housing and medical for you and your family... plus, the military offers exceptional opportunities to further your education and career, and it might turn out to be a wise choice. If you have a desire to travel, the military will usually see to it that you get to travel the world. Pay can rise significantly in your latter years due to years-in-service combined with promotional and educational opportunities, perhaps more so than any other career choice.

Keep in mind, discipline will play a large part of your daily activities and if you get mad at your superior, you can't just throw a tantrum or quit like you can in most other civilian careers. If you can accept orders and discipline, eventually you will be the one giving orders to others. The military has recruiting offices scattered about the country. They can assist you in selecting a military career, but be aware that they will give you tests to determine which career paths you are best suited for. If your desires don't match up with your abilities, you might not get the job you hoped for. You will also be required to undergo a complete physical and your initial commitment will be for several years.

Chapter 12 Self Employment

Self Employed: Working for yourself

You can also work for yourself, and especially if you're the go-getter type, you can reap huge rewards. It is possible to set your own hours and do your own thing. Keep in mind, though, that if you want to get and keep customers for your business, you might have to work on *their* time schedule, not necessarily yours. And it's not all cash in your pocket. Eventually, you will have to formally establish your business, and by this I mean that you might need to obtain a business license from your local or state authorities. You will also be expected to pay state, local and federal taxes on your business income, as well as personal taxes, such as income taxes on your take-home pay. Social Security and FICA taxes, business insurance, and a host of other sometimes necessary expenses such as unemployment insurance, etc. that would normally be paid or partially paid by your employer if you were working for someone else, are now your responsibility. These expenses can depend on your locale and type of business and whether you have any employees working for you, so you would need to investigate further what is required in your particular area.

All these business expenses eat into your earnings, leaving less available for your own personal take-home pay. Fortunately, most of these expenses are also tax-deductible when you file your income tax, and if you are doing a fair amount of business, you will probably find yourself filing income tax quarterly instead of annually. This information is not meant to frighten you away from starting your own business, because there's money to be made and freedom to choose your destiny by running your own business. Just be aware that there are things you must do, and rules you must follow, and things you must pay, so your actual take-home pay will not be equal to the weekly income from the business if you do everything legally. And you want to do everything legally.

Working for yourself is great, although working for another person's company sometimes gives you financial advantages in that medical insurance might be paid or partially paid, half of your Social Security and FICA will be paid, a 401k retirement plan or pension (either one with a company contribution as well as your own) might be available, so you will just have to weigh your own personal situation against available jobs and opportunities and determine whether you should work for someone else or strike out on your own.

Chapter 13 Education

Education: You might decide that you want to receive job training or further your education but the above-mentioned paths aren't available to you in your area. In that case, don't give up. There are other options you can pursue. We will talk about them in a minute, but first let's look at generalizations that could help advance your standing in any educational or career path.

One thing I would suggest is to read as much as possible about the type of work you think you want to do. Libraries are great places to find and absorb knowledge without the distractions of television, video games, and pesky siblings. The internet also offers a multitude of educational information, and I'm not talking about paid online tutoring. Instead, engineering forums, automobile and appliance repair forums, math, science, electronics, foreign language, biological sciences, whatever your interest and intended pursuit is, there is a surplus of information available at your fingertips. Of course, just because you saw it on the internet doesn't make this information totally accurate, but familiarization with the terms and job functions of your desired profession will give you a leg up against those who spend their internet time playing games.

Talking to people who are already working in the profession can give you a jump-start when you begin your education or career planning. That machinist uncle, for example, can teach you how to read a micrometer, the botanist can show you the various plants in his back yard and help you learn plant names and soil types, the environmental scientist can help you grasp human interaction with nature, etc. The point is to find out what these studies entail and what your job might be like before you commit time and money for your education, while also allowing you to become familiar with the subject before you ever sit down in a classroom. Your learning will be easier and more productive if you're already on track, and your instructor will appreciate the fact that you've shown initiative and are enthusiastic about your career education. Let's go check out Trade Schools.

Chapter 14 Trade Schools

Local Trade Schools: Typical Trade Schools teach the skills necessary to start out in your desired trade. Some are free, some have a tuition cost, and some that are state-sponsored might actually pay you a small stipend to attend. Most have a curriculum in the skilled trades, plus other career choices that are in demand.

Nursing is one class that is offered at a school near me. A friend's wife went for 18 months to get her LPN, then contracted with a local hospital to pay for her tuition and books to become a RN in return for a commitment to working at the hospital for two years after receiving her RN. All she had to do was ask and be willing to put in the hours.

Trade Schools often have Welding, HVAC, and Auto Mechanics classes as well as Information Technology and Cosmetology. Coming on strong are classes in Robotics and Mechatronics, a mixture of electronic and mechanical technologies. Sometimes classes fill up as quickly as they open for registration, so check it out and be ready to sign up when the next class becomes available. But before you commit yourself to a particular class at school, make sure that's what you want to do for a living. This applies to the college-bound student as well. Make sure this is what you want to do. If not, you are only wasting your time and money and also knocking someone else (with a genuine desire) out of that seat.

Class length at a Trade School depends on the course you are taking and can vary from about six months to over two years. This pretty much prevents you from working a fulltime day job, so you'll need to make arrangements to either live with your supportive parents, find a night job, or work part-time to earn money. Fortunately, many trade schools are now offering evening classes so that the students who do have a family or a full-time job can choose whichever class schedule suits their own personal situation.

Trade Schools may be listed by other names such as Industrial or Technical schools, or Colleges of Applied Technology.

Chapter 15 Community College

Community College: You might have to fork out some of your own money to attend, but here you can receive a two-year Associates Degree in the field of your choice. There are General Studies for those who aren't absolutely certain yet which curriculum they wish to follow, and in fact some learning paths have General Studies as a requirement. All colleges currently have their course catalogs on line, and you can examine them in the comfort of your home beforehand so you will have a better idea of what you are signing up for.

Some areas (my state included) provide free tuition for those first two years if you keep your grades up, attend regularly, and complete your classes. If your state does, that's a good deal for those who are determined to go to college. That's two years you won't have to pay for – or finance – your education. An associates degree from a community college can open many doors in the job market.

And by definition, these community colleges are located in or near communities that may be very close to your home. The advantage here is that you can (hopefully) still live at home and not have to rent an apartment far away. Mom and Dad will probably be willing to feed you and do your laundry for a couple more years as long as you stay in school and apply yourself. This fact alone could make community college a smart choice. Many employers are willing to adjust your work hours around your college schedule, allowing you to attend college without having to quit the local job you already have.

Before signing up to attend a local two-year college, make sure that your class credits will transfer to your preferred four-year college, if that is your goal. Many do, but some do not – especially if the two-year and the four-year colleges are located in different states.

Chapter 16 Four Year College

Four-year college: Back in my day, everyone was encouraged to attend college if at all possible, and we didn't even have Community Colleges in my area. The encouragement to attend college is still there today, and I acknowledge that college costs are enormous by comparison to the old days. So before you sign up for college, be sure and ask yourself this question: Is this what I actually want, or am I going to college until I can decide what I really want to do? If you're college-bound because you don't know yet what you want to do for the rest of your life, you might be making a big financial mistake. That's your choice, but a few things to consider first are these: Can I attend a community college or a local college where I can live and eat at home? Do I really want to incur a large debt, only to find out that college (or my chosen major) isn't for me? Will I be able to work a part-time job to help support myself? Plenty of college students do work a part-time job, either out of necessity or out of desire. Most of us aren't fortunate enough to be blessed with wealthy parents who are willing and able to shell out tens of thousands of dollars so we can have a free ride.

If you are borrowing your way through college, be sure and read the chapter on student loans, but no matter what, you should research scholarships and grants. In nearly all cases, scholarships won't fall from the sky and land in your lap. Sometimes a teacher will put your name in the pot for a scholarship, but usually, you will need to apply for yourself. Take advantage of every opportunity to apply. This is free money toward your education. Teachers and Guidance Counselors are good places to ask. Banks and Credit Unions sometimes give out scholarships to college-bound teens from the area. Sometimes trade unions will sponsor an employee's child or grandchild. Online resources are always a good place to check.

And don't forget to think along career lines when you're searching for financial help. If you are looking for a legal career, check with a nearby lawyer's office to see if they offer scholarships. If not they might consider giving a donation to help pay for your books, or hiring you for summer employment in their office. Looking for a medical career? Ask your doctor next time you're in for a checkup. Most doctors won't offer scholarships but many are willing to help sponsor a college-bound teen who shows an interest in the field. Veterinarian's office? Same deal. Ask, ask, ask. You might get a financial contribution or an offer of part-time work. The worst thing they can tell you is "No," but usually they will be able to offer helpful advice if not money. Sometimes their advice is worth more than a monetary contribution.

And please, if you are afforded free money through a donation, a grant, or a scholarship, use that money for college-related expenses and not for weekend vacations or parties with your friends. This will keep you from having to borrow so much for your education, money that you will be required to pay back... with interest.

Chapter 17 CO-OPs

Cooperative Education Programs and Internships: These programs offer the student who is attending college a chance to work in a real-world environment in their chosen field, while still being classified as a student. Some programs are a one-semester experience and some are alternating-semester work and study programs. Some of these programs (mostly Co-ops) will pay you while you work, and some do not. And while receiving pay for your work experience is a great benefit, an even greater benefit is the actual hands-on experience which usually lands the student a full-time position with the company upon graduation, because you already have knowledge and understanding of the company, the kind of work they do and the type work you will actually be doing once hired. Engineering students are most likely to be afforded this opportunity and often co-op in aerospace, petroleum, etc. industries. But even if your degree isn't engineering, you can still ask at the university you plan to attend about Co-ops and Internships. It never hurts to ask. Keep in mind that these Co-op and Internship programs are limited in the number of students who will be selected each year.

Chapter 18 GI Bill

GI Bill: If you have a parent in the Armed Forces, there is a chance that your parent qualifies for educational funding under the GI Bill. The GI Bill was designed to help veterans returning to civilian life obtain a higher education. Under some circumstances, the military parent can assign their GI Bill benefits to their child. That's right. If you have a military parent, you might be eligible to take advantage of this program.

There are a couple of caveats: You must maintain good grades and attendance records, and (This was recently in the news) if your parent assigns their GI Bill benefits to you, they may be obligated to serve an additional four years in the service. If they don't serve that extra time, then everything that was paid out on your behalf is due to be repaid, not by the parent, but by the student who benefitted from the military's disbursement of funds. So if your Dad gives you his GI Bill benefits and then retires one day before his additional four-year term is up, you could be required to pay back all the money for that free education you got, and suddenly it isn't free anymore. Make sure both you and your parent understand this stipulation before you sign up.

Chapter 19 Savings

Savings: It's never too early to begin saving. But saving for what? And how much should you save?

No matter how much you earn, it's all too easy for a teen or young adult to spend every dime they make. Movies, soda shops, parties, concerts, clothes, or even just hanging out, there are so many things to do, but all these things have an associated cost. Often, the cost of everything they want to do exceeds the income that allows them to do this. This is something you will have to figure out, but if your income won't stretch far enough, it usually comes down to this: you will need to either cut your spending or increase your income. Somewhere between the peer pressure of doing what the other kids do, and the adult behavior of being responsible with your money lies an easily obtained and adequate savings and spending program. I can promise that sooner or later, there's going to be a big expense. A necessary expense. Or even an emergency. If a teen spends everything they earn as they receive it, they're not going to have a backup fund. Let's get you to saving for both the short term and the long term, and it's not really painful, especially if it becomes a habit.

Saving doesn't have to be a proper savings account at the beginning, but can be a shoebox hidden in the closet or an envelope underneath the mattress. You can even use that old piggy bank from your childhood. Once you begin putting money in there every payday, and that pig gets heavier or that envelope gets fatter and fatter, you can envision the value of saving and accomplishing a financial goal. It's up to each person to decide how much to spend and how much to save. A good rule of thumb is to try and save 15% of your earnings, and that's probably a good place to start that will get you into an affordable lifelong habit of saving. If parents can afford to contribute matching or partially-matching funds to your account, then that can be seen as a reward for saving, and also as an incentive to encourage saving even more. That big TV, gaming console, bicycle, or whatever prize you want can be yours just by working part-time and saving a portion of your part-time earnings. These are known as short-term goals.

Once the part-time job becomes more of a full-time job, the teen can also begin saving toward more adult-oriented goals, such as when they buy their first car, get their own place, or begin post-secondary education. If they don't already have one, now might be a good time to open a proper savings account at a bank or credit union. It's generally safer than a shoebox. Now is also a good time to consider saving up an emergency fund and also saving for retirement. Retirement? That's a long way off and seems unimportant right now, but sooner or later it will become a significant objective. Age fifty? Too late to get started.

Age forty? Again too late. Thirty? Maybe. But if they begin with that first paycheck in their teens, saving will become a habit and not result in a crisis when they reach their 60s.

Let's see what a measly $25 a week can yield if you begin at age 18 and contribute that same $25 a week until you retire at age 67. For right now, we'll assume you earn an average rate of return of 7% (which is very high for a savings account in today's market, but might be a low number if invested in a mutual fund). Spreadsheets or online calculators will give you the following numbers, or you can solve using the formula I=Prt. Just add the contributions you make each year, plus the interest earned each year, back to your balance. The next time, calculate using your new balance as the Principal. Adding interest back to your balance and calculating your next year's interest on your new balance is known as the compounding of interest, where your money multiplies much faster. In this case, you will need to repeat this process nearly fifty times, but you will get there. This is where a calculator or a spreadsheet comes in handy, but regardless of how you make your calculations, you will find a surprise at the end.

That twenty-five dollars a week saved for 49 years - from age 18 to age 67 - at 7% interest will provide you with a half-million dollars at retirement! That's right, $500,000 at your retirement, just by cutting out $25.00 worth of burgers and fries each week. Of course, there might be fees (sometimes called a load) for your investment account. Some investment fees are a percent or more, but usually when there's a large group of people involved, as in a company-sponsored 401k, these fees are miniscule, way less than 1%. And imagine if, by the time you turn 30, you can finally afford to start putting away or investing $100 a week in place of that $25, suddenly that half-million dollars turns into well over a million dollars when you retire. In another scenario, fifty dollars a week for the entire time, from 18 to 67, will give you that same $1,000,000+

retirement fund. And don't forget, if the company you work for matches a portion of your retirement account, you can add that to the mix for an even greater retirement fund. Yep, it's conceivable that you can retire a millionaire. Congratulations!

You might think it will be impossible to scrounge an extra $25 a week, but perhaps - if you want to be realistic about it - it might just mean re-evaluating your priorities. You might be wasting that $25 or more a week and not even thinking about it. Here's an example of what I'm talking about:

An adult with several children stated that she was having trouble making her $250/month car payment. A question and answer session revealed that she had gotten into the habit of stopping at a drive-thru fast-food place every day after school to get sodas and snacks for her and the kids to "tide them over until dinner."

"It's only fifteen dollars," she said.

"Every day after school?"

"Yes, but it's only fifteen dollars," she said.

"There's twenty-something school days in a month," I said.

The light bulb lit up over her head and her look of despair vanished. She cracked a big, happy smile and as far as I am aware, she has not had any more money problems. That $300+ she was spending for after-school snacks every month was more than enough to make her car payment and was an unnoticed drain on her family budget. **Quite often, it is the little things that add up**.

So you will have to make the decision of how much to spend and how much to save, but the numbers we discussed should help illustrate the value of saving and also show what just a few dollars a day can add up to. When you think about it, that $25 a week we talked about saving, is only around $3.57 a day. That $50 per week is about $7.15 a day. Think you can't do it? I think you can, but if you insist that you can't, then perhaps all you need is a budget.

Chapter 20 The Budget

Oh, no! The dreaded budget.

If you cannot control money, then money will end up controlling you. If you still struggle each payday with deciding which portion of your money goes where, how can you possibly buy new shoes, how can you pay your phone bill, how can you save, then you should think about a written budget. Remember our discussion about writing down where we've spent our money and how much? Well, a written budget is similar in concept, but instead of writing down where we've already spent our money, we can write down where we're *going* to spend our money. Yep, each dollar is assigned a place to go before we turn loose of any money, or even better, before we ever cash that paycheck. A typical budget for a young teen with a part-time job might look something like the following list:

Pay:	$65/ week
Phone bill:	$80/ month, or $20/ week
Car insurance:	$100/ month or $25/ week
Savings:	$10/ week
Emergency:	$5/ week
Gasoline:	$12/ week
Eating out or Movie:	$25/ week
Clothing:	$10/ week

In short, you pre-determine where your money is going to go - every dollar - and then you stick with it. If you begin by listing your fixed and absolutely necessary monthly expenses, then follow with your variable and discretionary spending, you will have a grasp of where your money is directed. Notice we left some money in the budget for eating out or going to a movie, so you will still be able to enjoy the fruits of your labor. If you noticed in the example budget above that your weekly expenses exceed your weekly income, then congratulations to you for catching that! You wrote it down beforehand and now you can see that your money will not go far enough to carry you through the week. So what can we do about that?

We'll need to trim our spending, or we'll need to generate more income. One or the other, or perhaps both. It's easy to see once it is written down - on paper - in front of you. Obviously, your car insurance needs to be paid, and your phone bill as well, but seeing on paper that your phone bill eats up nearly a third of your income, you might want to investigate how to reduce that bill. If your current phone arrangement is locked into a contract or is all-to-important to you that you aren't willing to make changes there, then you will need to make cuts somewhere else. Should we cut money alloted to Savings or Emergency? No, it is imperative that we have some back-up money, and we'll get to that real soon. Gasoline? Perhaps we could cut there, but if you use $12 worth of gasoline going back and forth to work and school every week, we can't really make cuts there, either.

Reality is now setting in, and we realize... by looking at our written budget... that we need to reduce our entertainment budget or our clothing budget in order to survive the week, but the fact that totally eliminating both these items will still leave us a few dollars short of balancing our budget, we are now faced with re-addressing our phone arrangements or earning more money. It's your choice, but at least our written budget has shown us what needs to be done. And it wasn't hard, was it?

I know without asking that some of you really wanted to cut out your Savings and Emergency contributions to that shoebox or account, but let's see why we need to have it.

Let us assume you have a flat tire, the tire is ruined, and you need to buy a new one. That's what the emergency fund is for.

"But I can't buy a tire for $5.00" you say.

No, you can't. But if you have been working for several months and putting back that $5 per week, every week, you probably have enough saved to buy a new tire. That's if you consider a new tire to be an actual emergency, and it is if you rely on your vehicle to take you to work and school. Getting your hair done or purchasing that new video game when it first comes out are not emergencies. But if your car is your only way to get around, fixing or replacing the tire on your car is an actual emergency. After buying that new tire, you can begin putting back that $5 again, so that later when another emergency arises, you'll be able to handle it without going into crisis mode or borrowing money from that corner quick-cash place. See how easy it is to budget, even for unforseen circumstances? Instead of scrambling or panicking every week when you run out of money, you have it all planned out, and barring any *huge* unexpected expenses, you already have a sense of where your money is going and you can handle a small emergency.

Your budget will be dynamic and subject to change as your income and needs change. You may end up with a larger or smaller paycheck beginning next month, or you might just incur new expenses along the way. And after this discussion, if you ultimately arrive at the conclusion that you will adjust your budget so that you eliminate your savings and emergency monies so you can have more money to spend for movies, popcorn, burgers and fries, feel free to do so. You're not fooling me, you are only fooling yourself.

Know that as you get older, things change. Grownups, and especially those with families, have an entirely different set of priorities in their budget. Adulting will do that to you. I could list a thousand places where a parent's money needs to go, things like diapers, formula, doctor bills, car payments, car repairs, rent, groceries, electric bill, house insurance, fixing the refrigerator, braces for the kids... the list of expenses goes on and on and on and seems like it will never end. The magnitude and cost of emergencies are greatly increased as well when you are an adult. Getting into a habit of budgeting and saving at a young age can certainly help prepare you for handling money when you're on your own, starting a family, or just being grown up.

Try it and see how it works out for you.

Chapter 21 Investing

Investing: Investing is the act of allocating money with the expectation of returning a profit. That could mean anything from flipping houses to buying stocks and bonds. We'll stick with investing as it relates to long-term money investments, and I'll be the first to admit I have lost plenty of money in the stock market, mainly by thinking I could outsmart the professional traders and pick winning stocks all by myself. I was wrong and I lost a lot of money. Unless you possess an innate sense of what's going to be the next big thing, I don't think you should do it, but that's just my opinion based on my own personal experience. For the long-term investor, it's hard to beat the historical returns associated with having some of your money invested in the market, and nowadays, I think it's better to let a pro manage a mutual fund (bundle of assorted stocks) for you rather than try to do it yourself. The stock market and other similar investments usually go up and down on a daily basis, but over time, generally show a positive return.

There are several largely accepted ways to invest money for retirement, and these usually have their origins within the Internal Revenue code. Let's look at a few of these.

Chapter 22 Long Term Investing

401k, SEP, Roth, Pension: Long term investment/Retirement programs. What does this all mean?

If you are just starting out, these terms will have little meaning or significance to you, but once you are established in your lifetime occupation, you will want to one day sit down and think about saving for - not the immediate things - but for your far-off future. We will briefly touch on a few available ways to save and invest long-term. These are all retirement plans or IRAs - Individual Retirement Accounts. Each has its own distinguishing features and sometimes more than one of these plans can apply to you.

As I said, these plans will probably not interest you if you are still in your teens or early twenties, but the sooner you get started, the more time that compound interest will have to multiply your money. We've already seen how Time affects the amount of Interest you'll need to pay back if you *borrow* money (and we'll look at that again later) but that same Time can also compound the interest you will accumulate on your savings if you put it there and leave it there. That's how our $25 per week example a few chapters back turned out to be a half-million dollar pile of money when you retire. If you elect to participate in one of these plans, you can usually change your contribution amounts once each year. The fact that you can change your contributions annually will allow you to eventually find a good balance between your annual spending requirements and your annual savings desires.

Take note that ALL established retirement plans have rules and restrictions. There are contribution limits, withdrawal restrictions, etc. that you should be aware of before joining. Especially important is the fact that once you put that money in there, you **cannot** get it out before a certain age (usually 59 ½) without paying huge penalties. Some plans offer the option to borrow money from your retirement account if you find yourself in a financial pinch, but resist the urge. If certain conditions are met, such as you leaving your job or getting laid off while you have an outstanding loan, you could discover that the entire amount you borrowed would be considered a distribution from your account and is due and payable immediately, or you could find that you're responsible for taxes and penalties on the amount still to be paid back to your account. Study the plan information your company or plan administrator furnishes and ask questions if you don't understand. Most companies will have selected a firm to manage their accounts, and most firms offer choices of how you want your money to be invested such as stocks, bonds, a mixture of both, etc. You should learn all you can about these types of funds before you invest in them.

Realize that there's always the possibility that Congress could change the terms of any retirement plan that is based on Internal Revenue code. One would expect that if changes are made, an existing plan and its participants would be grandfathered in and maintain the existing terms of their plan, while newcomers would be required to abide by any new terms. That's the good and the bad. Now let's take a closer look at the individual features of those retirement plans.

Chapter 23 The 401(k)

401(k) is named for the Internal Revenue code that allows an employer to set up a retirement savings plan for its employees. 401(k) plans are tax-deferred plans. This means that any contributions you make - and any contributions your employer contributes on your behalf - are not taxable when you earn this money, but instead are taxed when you withdraw the money, usually after you are retired. Anything you contribute to your 401(k) is subtracted from your income before you file your income tax, and that reduced income will be noted on your W2 form; therefore you end up paying less income tax each year to the IRS. Remember that you will be paying taxes on this money when you withdraw it. **With**

a 401(k) you save taxes on the front end, but pay taxes on the back end.

Although contributions to a 401(k) are made each pay period, for simplicity's sake, suppose you contribute $1,000 this year to your 401(k). You will not pay taxes on that $1,000 when you file your income taxes for this year, thus saving $120 if you are in a 12% bracket. In effect, you have saved a thousand dollars and only reduced your take-home pay by $880 ($1,000 - $120 = $880).

When you retire, if that $1,000 has grown to a million dollars, you will pay taxes on that million dollars as you withdraw it. Of course, you won't withdraw it all at once, but whatever portion you do withdraw, you will pay taxes on it (it will be treated as ordinary income) for that year, at the current rate for your tax bracket.

Chapter 24 The Roth IRA

The Roth IRA is similar in concept, but the money that goes into your Roth account is taxed when you get paid, but after that, you'll never pay another dime's worth of tax on that money or the money it earns in your account. Imagine if you invest a thousand dollars today like we did for our 401(k) and it's worth the same million dollars when you retire, that entire million dollars can be withdrawn totally tax-free. You already paid taxes of $120 when you earned that thousand dollars, if you are in a 12% bracket, but will pay no more taxes when you withdraw from your Roth account. **With a Roth IRA you pay taxes on the front end and save paying taxes on the back end.** Some employers offer one or more of the retirement savings plans mentioned, and you should think about participating as many as you can, especially as far as any employer-match is concerned. That employer match is free money.

Some companies still offer traditional pensions as well, although they are falling out of favor. But if a pension is offered, it might be smart to join. Usually, the company also contributes some of their own money to the pension plan, and again, who wants to turn down free money?

This is as simple as it gets, although in reality, it's more complicated than that. A financial planner would probably judge the value a dollar today against the expected value of a dollar in 40 or 50 years. In addition, they would also take into account the *anticipated* tax bracket you will be in when you retire. It is impossible to know what these numbers will be when you do retire and begin withdrawing money from your account, but I will say that if you have both a 401(k) and a Roth, you have reduced your taxes somewhat when you got paid, and you can pick and choose how much to withdraw out of each account during your retirement years to minimize your tax burden.

Chapter 25 The SEP

The SEP is a Simplified Employee Pension plan and is normally used by someone who works for themselves or owns a small business. If you work for yourself and do not have access to a company-sponsored 401(k) or a Roth IRA, you might want to set up your own SEP. You can choose from pre-designed investment plans or create your own, within approved guidelines. This might be a good choice if you are a sole proprietor and want to save toward your retirement.

Many self-employed persons choose to sell their business when they retire. They consider their business to be their retirement fund. For many people this works out well, but for others whose business has faded from popularity, this can be a catastrophe. An example would be the person who runs a typewriter sales and service business. Business was once booming, but now... not so much demand for typewriters anymore. So an SEP would be a financial cushion for this person.

Chapter 26 Borrowing Money

Borrowing money: So far we have spent money, saved money, and invested money. But what if we need to borrow money? We have already touched on short-term loans and seen what effect interest rates and time have on our payback. Sometimes, we have to borrow money for the long term to finance a big purchase such as a house or a car. While some fortunate people are able to pay cash for these type purchases, most of us are not and will have to seek out a large loan for an extended length of time. We will look at borrowing for that big purchase in a minute.

Before you borrow, you should feel confident that your job is secure and your credit rating is good. With that said, now might be a good time to look at our credit rating.

Chapter 27 Credit Ratings

Credit Ratings: I can assure you that billionaires don't give a hoot about their Credit Report. But you should. That report only shows that you've been borrowing money, and that you have, or have not, been paying it back in a timely manner, but these things matter to someone who is about to entrust you with their money. Your report may also show if your money has been attached (paying money you owe through a legal process). It is a sad state of affairs that you will have to borrow money and pay it back in order to prove that you are trustworthy enough to borrow money and pay it back, but that's the way the system works. And the system doesn't care if you've been injured and can't work, you've lost your job, or for whatever reason you are behind in payments. They only report that you are current and have been timely (high score), or that you've been lax in making payments or have missed payments, or that your consumer debt is already too high compared to your income. (lower score). Ultimately, your credit score will help prospective lenders determine your ability and desire to pay them back, and will also help determine whether you get a low-interest loan or a high-interest loan. Remember when we gave examples of high vs. low interest rates on credit cards?

I am not suggesting that a teen or young adult rush out and get a credit card just to build up a credit rating. I am only suggesting that when they do get that card, they should be responsible and make adequate and timely payments. Do not miss a payment.

I will also tell you that if you go online and check your credit report, you will soon begin receiving credit card offers from every credit company in the universe. Apparently there is a trigger in the system that tells these people you might be interested in applying for more credit, and they can't wait to tempt you with offers. Resist, these places are only trying to entice you with offers you can't refuse so they can get their claws into your money.

***

Now back to borrowing…

The best thing I can say when shopping for a loan is that you should probably first approach your local bank or credit union where you have already established a checking and/or a savings account. They will be more likely to give you a reasonably-priced loan than a company you just made friends with online. The local institution already has your records, they know how much money you have accumulated and how frequently you put money in and take money out. In short, they are probably your best bet for a small loan or to obtain a credit card. They might even be your best bet for a car loan or a loan to purchase your home.

Online mortgage lenders have been coming on strong recently and competing with local banks for your business, but it is nice to have a storefront to walk into when you have a question or need to transact business. My opinion is that until you are experienced with borrowing money and paying it back, you are better off with a local bank or credit union.

There are other local resources available when you need to borrow money. Let's look at another source of accessible money.

In all likelihood you will find on a street corner in your town, a quick money, fast money, title-money or similarly-named entity that wants to lend you money. My view is this: If you are serious about being in charge of your hard-earned money, you should shy away from these places. They serve a genuine purpose, which is this: they give quick access to a small amount of cash for a short period of time for those who have no other option. Other than that, in my opinion, they serve no purpose for someone who wants to get ahead. And in fact, if you have saved a small percentage of your money as we have previously suggested, you (hopefully) shouldn't need to use one of these places when a crisis arrives. These should be a last-ditch, real-life financial emergency situation, no-other-choice source of quick cash. Again, that's just my opinion. If you do actually have to use one of these lending places, make it a one-time visit and pay it back, do not make it a habitual place to visit just because they are convenient. The interest rates plus fees can be astronomical, plus you are actually pledging your car as collateral at a lot of these places. If you don't pay, they come take your car and then have the nerve to charge you for hauling it away. I'm serious.

I once had a stack of papers tossed in front of me. "I can't pay these. Can you help me figure out what's wrong?" The first thing I noticed from the paper on top of the pile was a quick-cash loan with an Effective Interest Rate of 127%. One hundred twenty seven percent! That ought to be illegal, but here's the thing about "Effective Interest Rates". This is the actual interest rate, plus origination fees, plus loan servicing fees plus whatever else they can think of to add on to your obligation. It reflects the actual total cost of your loan.

Let's compare a one-thousand dollar loan at 127% against a 15% bank loan. Remember our formula, I=Prt?

Interest = $1,000 * 1.27 * 1 = $1,270

You will have to pay back the original $1,000 plus an additional $1,270 interest. Your total payback for a year-long loan is $2,270. For this calculation we assumed simple interest, calculated only once.

That same loan at a bank or Credit Union at 15% is this:

Interest = $1,000 * .15 * 1 = $150

You will have to pay back your original $1,000 plus an additional $150. Your total payback is $1,150. In this case, you have saved $2,270 - $1,150 = $1,120 on this one short-term loan by shopping your bank or credit union. Of course, there may be a slight fee for processing your paperwork at the bank or credit union, but if so, it will be miniscule by comparison.

Typically though, a short-term loan is just that - short term, so if you financed for only six months, your interest paid back would be equal to about one half that of the year-long loans above. The calculations made above are a good example of how we can use our Interest formula I= Prt to be informed about the costs of borrowing money. Always remember that when you borrow money, they expect you to pay them back. If you don't, they will find you and prosecute you, and by the time you pay what you owe plus legal fees and court costs (plus that I=Prt interest that keeps accumulating up until the day the judge hears the case) you will find yourself paying much more than your original debt. Be smart. Pay your obligations.

Chapter 28 That First Car

Vroom Vroom: Sooner or later you will start driving, and then before you know it, you'll be wanting your own car or your parents will get tired of hauling you and your friends around and insist you find your own set of wheels. So let's talk about that first car.

Some teens will be fortunate enough to obtain a free hand-me-down car or truck from a friend or relative, but most will find it necessary to buy their own. In either case, it's important that some ground rules be set before you ever get behind the steering wheel. And remember, we're talking about money here. The safety rules, driving restrictions, and curfews are up to you, your parents, and the state in which you live.

One axiom is that teens seem to take better care of their car if they are financially invested in the vehicle. I believe that to be true. Even if the car was a gift, there are a few expenses you can pay for to ensure that you have some of your own money tied up in the vehicle. Registration, tax, tags, insurance, maintenance and repairs, fuel, tires and wiper blades… any of these are things you might accept responsibility for. Insurance is a big-ticket item when you start driving, and you and your parents should probably talk to your automobile insurance agent before you decide on what car to purchase. Maybe you want a swoopy red race car, but when you find out that the insurance is unobtainable or exceeds your annual income, perhaps it's time to delay that race car purchase and discuss the pursuit of a more modest type of vehicle.

Cars can be found through word-of-mouth, sitting in yards, on street corners, in newspaper ads and on dealership lots. Almost always, the asking price is not the lowest-dollar selling price. Feel free to try your hand at negotiating a lower price. The worst thing they can say is "No," and you can choose to either walk away or raise your offer. It's also a good idea to have an experienced person with you who can point out any defects you might have missed, or you might want to have the car checked over by a mechanic. Most used cars are sold "As-Is" and you don't want the newfound joy of ownership to be ruined by purchasing a car that needs thousands of dollars in repairs.

Now that you're ready to buy your first car, do you know how you'll pay for it? If you don't have enough cash, you will need to borrow money.

Chapter 29 The Pity Party

The PITY PARTY: The financing of a car is probably a good time to discuss throwing youself a pity party, so we will insert that right here. The PITY party is not what it sounds like, but is actually a time of joy and celebration. PITY is an acronym for Prove It To Yourself, and it's not exclusive to automobiles; it can apply to any large financed purchase. Here's how it works, and it is simple in execution:

Before you commit to that expensive purchase, prove that you can make the payments. That shiny car, that first apartment, that expensive video gaming system… If you are going to be required to make monthly payments, prove it to yourself – and your parents – that you can indeed afford these payments. An example is this: You want that car of your dreams, but it's going to cost you $500 a month for five years to make those payments. If you think it's going to be easy making those payments, then prove it. Prove it to yourself. Put that $500 a month into your savings for six months.

Then if your monthly financial situation is still comfortable, if you can survive without that $500 a month for six months, then perhaps you are ready to commit to those payments for a longer term. The positive aspect is that you now have $3,000 saved up toward a down payment ($500 x 6 = $3,000), you won't have to finance quite so much, and you have proven to yourself (and your parents) that you can swing the purchase. You can now have that PITY party.

If you can't comfortably save that $500 a month for six months, then you should now realize that you cannot afford that particular purchase. You will need to reevaluate your situation and find a way to either generate more income, decrease your everyday spending or find a less expensive car. The good thing is you haven't committed yourself to a 60 month contract that you can't fulfill, and you have hopefully accumulated some money in the process. In any case, be aware that life does happen. Loss of a job, a business closing, hospital bills… any of these can pop up at any time without notice, and dump your best-laid plans right into the trash can. It happens.

But if you're ready to finance that automobile now, there's a few things to be aware of. Although some do, most dealers do not actually finance their cars through the dealership, but rather contract with different lending institutions to find someone who is willing to take the risk of your ability to pay them back. The dealer fills out the paperwork and submits it to the bank, and very soon you will be approved or disapproved. This is one place your credit rating comes into play. If you are approved, all the legal paperwork as far as registration, licensing, etc. is usually (but not always) completed by the dealer and submitted to either your state or county office, and soon you are on your way home with your car. Oh wait! You are at least eighteen years old, right?

If not, the car will need go into your parent's name in many cases. If you're a minor, you may need to hitch a ride on your parent's automobile insurance as well until you age a few years. And there's a probability that your parent will have to co-sign those loan papers too, which makes your parents responsible to make the payments if you don't. Hopefully, you have already impressed your parents with your money habits and they feel you are responsible enough to take on this obligation. Do not let your parents down.

If all this sounds overwhelming, you might want to find a $3,000 car to start out with and forego all the paperwork involved with financing a car. After all, who wants to pay interest money on something that depreciates every day, anyway? Remember that money you saved for your PITY party? Perhaps you have enough saved to buy a "starter" vehicle and won't need to finance anything. If so, be sure that the title and paperwork you receive with your cash car is free and clear and proper for the state in which you live. This will prevent headaches when you go to register the vehicle in your name. Best of luck whichever way you decide to go. Drive safely and enjoy your car.

Chapter 30 Moving Out

Housing: Oh no, another expense

Most likely, the teen still resides with their parents. And they probably should if possible, at least until they make it through school or a training program, have a good job, and are emotionally and financially strong enough to strike out on their own. Then before moving out, there are many things to consider, things like should you be renting, sharing, owning, etc.

The following chapters are to make you aware of some things you should consider before you commit to moving into your own place. The fact that Mom and Dad have been paying for your housing, providing you with internet and cable TV, keeping the house warm in winter and cool in summer, cooking your meals, washing the dishes, washing and ironing your clothes, keeping the pantry and refrigerator stocked, and a multitude of other behind-the-scene functions should not go unnoticed. They usually do these things and pay these bills without bringing them to your attention, but once you are out on your own, somebody will need to take care of these items, and that somebody is you. These things require a commitment of time, labor and money.

Chapter 31 Renting a Place

Rent. This is the teen or young adult living in someone else's house or apartment and paying money for that privilege. Rental properties often come with some amenities included. Some provide a few or all of these things: Electric, cable, water, sewer, garbage pickup, parking, yard care, maintenance and repair. Some provide none of these things. Some come furnished and some do not. Some have kitchen appliances and some do not. Many are a lease property, often requiring a 12 month lease that rolls over to a month-to-month tenancy after 12 months. Some will allow you to have a pet, some do not. Whatever you do, discuss these things and read and understand the entire contract **before** you sign any papers. One thing that every landlord requires is money. Often, the first month's rent

+ the last month's rent + a security deposit that will be used to repair any damage you do or be applied to any back rent that you owe. An individual property owner with one rental house may not run a background or credit check on potential renters, but you can be sure that a person who rents properties as their main source of income will check everything. Make sure your background check/credit rating comes back clean.

Remember when we talked about savings? Well, here's an example where some of your savings might come in handy. Moving into a new place is costly, so be prepared. As we just mentioned, some things are included and some are not. The ones that are not included will require you to lay out some cold, hard cash. Utility companies will require you to put down a deposit on your water, electric, gas, etc. and they want these deposits before they will ever turn your utilities on. Furniture, appliances, dishes, soap, towels, groceries, all these things that a teenager or young adult takes for granted while living at home may not be there at your new place. You will need to buy a lot of stuff. Save some of your money for this day of independent living. And pay your rent on time.

Some young adults move out of their parent's house and into a rental or leased property that they intend to *share* with someone else. This can be a great plan for cutting expenses if everyone gets along and everyone is committed to sharing the bills. The downside of this situation is that personal conflicts can arise, one of you can lose their source of income, one of you moves out, or someone just refuses to pay their share. These problems do occur, and if your name is on the paperwork and your roommate cannot pay or refuses to pay, or cannot be located, you and you alone will most likely be responsible for paying the entire rent and utility bills all by yourself. Think about this before you agree to share a place with someone. If you do share, have an agreed-upon exit strategy in place just in case one of you decides to leave.

Chapter 32 Buying a House

Buying your own house. Not everyone wants to rent; some desire home ownership. Many young adults purchase their first home when they leave the nest. Is this good for every teen or young adult? Not necessarily, as every person's situation is different. But here are a few things to think about.

Appreciation: Generally, but not always, homes appreciate in value over time. This increases the equity in your home, meaning for example, if you bought a $150,000 home a few years ago and now homes in that neighborhood have increased in value by 10%, your home's worth has increased by (150,000 x .10= 15,000) $15,000. Your home is now worth $165,000 and you never did anything but live there and maintain it. Wow!

But don't forget… you have to maintain it, meaning that you may have paid out $8,000 for a new roof and $4,000 for a new A/C unit during those few years, typically expenses that you would not have to pay if you were renting. Same for termite treatments and lawn maintenance and a host of other expenses. And sometimes homes do depreciate. For example, if a major employer in the area shuts down, or a military base nearby closes, homes may sag in value. Be aware and evaluate your own surroundings. If you do decide to purchase, you should be mindful of some of the costs and terms associated with the purchase of that new home.

Mortgage: Simply put, a mortgage is a legal agreement in which your bank lends you money to buy a property, and holds title to that property until you have paid them in full.

Amortization: This is another term you should become familiar with. Amortization is defined as paying back your loan. You make a payment to the lending institution, and once they have it, they divide your payment into two groups: the amount paid toward the principal and the amount paid for interest. Amortization calculators can be found in spreadsheets or online. These calculators will produce a chart, and this chart will enable you to visualize how your payment money is allocated each month. Since you are this far along in the book, you should not be surprised to discover that the lending institution grabs a big chunk of their interest money out of your payment first, with very little of your money going toward paying down the principal. As the years go by, their part slowly decreases and your part slowly increases. The amounts you pay for taxes and insurance are not shown on the amortization chart, but are deposited into a separate account, generally called an Escrow Account, and are withdrawn and paid by the bank when these bills are due.

A sample amortization chart can be found in the appendix, showing disbursements for both principal and interest.

Down payment. Typically, you will be required to make a down payment when you buy a home. Usually, 10% is acceptable. Great deal, but an even better deal is if you can pay 20% (or more) down. One reason for that is that you will be financing – and paying interest on – only 80% of the purchase price, rather than 90%. You're spending less money every month for your house payment. Yet another reason is that most lending institutions will require **PMI** on anything less than a 20% down payment. So what is PMI? PMI is Private Mortgage Insurance. The bank wants some assurance that you will stay in your house and make payments on a timely, regular basis, and they feel that if you have some skin in the game (your own money) you'll be less likely to skip out and leave them with a property to dispose of. If you don't follow through with your part of the contract, that PMI will help the bank out. That's understandable, they're protecting their own interest, but they are perfectly willing to let you pay for it. Once again, the lending institution allows you to pay for their protection. So if you can make a 20% down payment, you save money on finance charges plus you aren't paying for PMI. Win, win. If you do find yourself paying PMI, know that it usually ceases whenever the LTV (Loan to Value) ratio drops below 80%. This can be accomplished in a couple of ways. One, you can pay down your mortgage until you owe less than 80% of its value, or two, the value of your house rises until what you owe is less than 80% of the value. Or, a combination of both. Many times, you will have to ask your financing institute to drop the PMI once your LTV is below 80%, as many times they don't volunteer to do this.

I must insert here that at the time this is written, some would argue that 10% down + paying PMI might be a better deal for the homebuyer. Their thought process is that houses are rising in value so quickly that by the time you save up an additional 10% towards a down payment, housing values - and thus the payments - will have risen more than the additional cost of paying PMI.

I cannot argue with them except to say this depends on many factors such as the area where you are buying, how fast you are saving, etc. Either way, the bank gets your money, but the choice is ultimately yours.

Some home loans are available with as little as 3-5% down (FHA Loans) or even Zero% down (USDA Loans). There are certain buyer qualifications and certain property qualifications that must be met. Sometimes you might even be able to let the seller pay your down payment for you if they are willing. But keep in mind the more you finance, 100% vs. 80%, the higher your payments will be, interest rates being equal.

Appraisal: The bank wants to know what the house is worth so they will know how much they can comfortably lend to you. You get to pay for this. And it's likely that a home inspection will be required as well. Once again, you get to pay, this time to evaluate someone else's house.

Property Taxes and Insurance: While you are the one paying your property taxes and insurance, most often your lending institution will require that you pay those expenses to them (and include these in your house payment each month), and they will in turn pay out the money to your insurance company and county tax collector. Generally, they will collect 1/12 the estimated annual amount each month and then pay these items when due each year. They have their money tied up in financing your house and want to be 100% certain that these important bills are paid. After your house is paid off, the responsibility falls into your lap to pay these items. You should know what these costs are and be prepared to pay them when due, because they usually amount to thousands of dollars per year.

Closing costs. Closing costs are payments to either a third party or the bank's own in-house paper-shufflers and are disbursed as necessary. These costs usually cover attorney's fees, payoff of the seller's existing

126

loan, taxes, deed recording fees, realtor commissions, and other miscellaneous fees all lumped under the heading of Closing Costs. You will be given a Settlement Sheet or settlement statement that breaks down the individual costs.

Title Insurance. Title insurance is payment for someone to go to your local records office and look through the history of deeds, transfers and liens on the property you are buying to ensure that there are no other persons who can make a claim on the property; that the property is free and clear of any encumbrances. You can actually do this search yourself, for free in the majority of cases, but having a Title Company do this is cheap insurance… if anything unnoticed comes up a year or a decade from the time of your purchase, the title company is supposed to make things right.

There are plenty of other costs associated with buying and financing and moving into your home, including other lender fees, furniture, appliances, utility deposits, moving expenses, etc. In summary, it is quite expensive to move into your first house, but depending on a number of factors such as your area, your income, your desire to live there, and whether or not you plan to remain in that locale for a long time, it might be a good investment. If you're not settled into your career yet, or are not sure where you want to make your permanent home, perhaps you should consider renting. The choice is yours. However you select your new residence, whether you rent or buy, know that somewhere along the way, your credit rating will likely come into play when arranging for your new residence.

Chapter 33 Student Loans

Student Loans: Probably the largest expenditure you will ever make is buying your home. A close second, at least for some, is the Student Loan.

I find it odd that a hard-working teenager with $5,000 of earned money in the bank, his own car that he's paid for, and a desire to open his own business has trouble borrowing $25,000 to finance his startup, yet a same-aged kid with no work experience, no money, and no credit history can easily borrow two or three times that amount to go to college. Think about that. It is wrong on so many levels, yet here we are.

Most teens today, if they do pursue college, will have to borrow money at some point during their learning years. There should be no embarrassment about that.

College is expensive. But do you need to borrow all they will let you borrow? Do you need to finance everything?

Before you start borrowing money, you should exhaust every single option for free money that you can. Scholarships, grants, gifts, whatever source of free money you can chase, chase it! And hopefully, if you're college bound, you've been saving some of your own money toward your higher education. Any dollar that you don't have to borrow for school today could be worth two or three dollars or more a decade after you graduate.

I will stop right here and state that I do not have, nor have I ever had a student loan, and I would recommend you seek professional advice if you have questions. So why am I addressing student loans if I've have never had one? Because I have seen suffering and frustration from many around me who have been stupid with their money. Absolutely stupid. And now they are bitter about that student loan albatross around their neck. And for the most part, at least the ones I'm familiar with, it's all their own ignorant fault... ignorance in this case not being a derogatory term, but meaning uninformed and perhaps careless. It's their money habits that are stupid.

I'll start with an example of the poor habits I'm talking about. This is a college student with a part-time job nine months out of the year and a full forty-hour-a-week job during the summer. Scholarships and grants aren't enough to cover all college expenses, but this student does receive a considerable amount of free money. That free money (as much as is available for non-accountable expenditures), is used for concerts, dining out, expensive coffees, condos on the beach for Spring Break, and a cabin in the mountains for Fall Break. Hanging with her friends. Part-time job pays for new phones, clothes, gas to ride the roads, more dining out, new hairdos, getting nails done, and plenty more frivolous spending, obviously habits left over from those freewheeling teenage high school days. Borrows nearly everything for school expenses. If you are astute, you already know where this is going, but for those who haven't quite caught on, student loans eventually totaled over $50,000. This student probably could have paid most of that college expense with her free money and her part-time earnings over four years. But she borrowed for her education while living at home where the food was free, the rent was free, and the only expenses she had were of her own choice such as phone bill, etc. Fast forward a couple of decades. She no longer lives at home and now has rent, utilities, grocery bills and other living expenses, she struggles to pay the minimum amount on her loan, and her outstanding student loan debt has grown to nearly $135,000… almost three times her original loan!

Now we have to wonder why. This lady has a well-paying job and has been (according to her) paying back her loan consistently. Or has she?

Let's take a look. She actually has been paying (but only the minimum amount) since she began payback (except for that deferrment when she went back to school for a while) and she has also re-financed her loan to get a better interest rate. So what went wrong?

Remember that I=Prt formula? It bit her in the butt, partly because the lending institution calculates interest on a daily basis and partly because she did not pay attention to her money. Yep, she pays over $250 per month toward her student loan, but her monthly interest charge alone is more than what she pays every month. And of course, the lending institution grabs their interest payment first every month, then if there's anything left, it is applied to the principal. But in this case, there's nothing extra to pay down the principal, so the amount she owes on the principal never goes down, but the interest she owes continues to grow every month, until.... There's a thing called Capitalization, and in this case, capitalization refers to the lending institution's ability to roll the interest over to the principal. Capitalization of student loans, as I understand it, can occur when any of a number of designated actions occur, such as failing to make a payment, refinancing the loan, deferring payments, etc. Any of these actions can trigger the capitalization of your interest, and now your principal balance is even higher and your payments are higher, and right about now is when you wish you hadn't borrowed so much money. I promise you that if you don't pay attention to your money, you can easily find yourself in the same situation.

Lending Institutions are in the business to make money, make no mistake about that. They will get theirs eventually. And the longer it takes, the more they are due to receive because that interest keeps on accumulating. Some older people living on Social Security are still paying on their student loans. Think about that. Do you want to still be paying for your education when you are sixty or seventy years old? It would seem that the wise student would borrow the least amount necessary to accomplish their higher education goals, and then pay it back as quickly as possible, and paying more than the minimum required each time. (If you are on a PSLF plan, you might not want to pay extra) However, check your lending institution's policies.

Sometimes, you have to actually designate that the extra money you are paying goes toward the principal, otherwise they will scrape their interest portion off the top. Some have a prepayment penalty and some do not. Some will suspend interest accumulation if you go back to school and some will not. Before you sign on the dotted line, or if you have already signed on the dotted line, you need to know and understand what the terms of your contract are. Find out, then develop a plan to pay off your student loan, and pay it off as soon as possible. Otherwise, you could be paying for the rest of your life.

I want to reiterate something I said a few pages back: "Any dollar that you don't have to borrow for school today could be worth two or three dollars or more a decade after you graduate."

To expound on that and put it into perspective, any $10,000 you don't have to borrow for school today could be worth $20,000 or $30,000 or more that you won't have to pay back a decade after you graduate.

Chapter 34 Giving

Giving: Helping Others

It's a personal thing, but I think there's no better joy than to give. It makes you feel whole, or more complete inside. How much you choose to give (or can afford to give) is a personal matter, and that choice does not always mean money. If you can't afford to give money or choose not to, perhaps you can afford to donate some of your personal time to a worthy cause, or help an individual in your own neighborhood by doing a chore they are unable to do. Someone, somewhere, will appreciate what you have contributed and you will definitely feel better about yourself. Just try to give something.

Churches, civic organizations, neighborhood associations, local or national fundraisers, children's hospitals… there are many places you can find to contribute and where you can make a difference in someone else's life.

Chapter 35 Summary

For most of us, building wealth is not an overnight achievement but a long and sometimes tedious journey. It takes planning and dedication, things often missing from a teenager's daily ruminations. Though each of us will have a different definition of wealth and have our sights set on different goals, we all have to start somewhere.

Hopefully, this introductory book has opened your eyes to a basic understanding of money, and has pointed out the value of spending, saving, and borrowing wisely. Perhaps more eye-opening were the examples of real-life money traps you can easily fall prey to when you don't pay attention to your money.

Books abound on each and every subject covered here, and although I have read and studied many of them, most are lengthy (sometimes hundreds of pages or more) explanations that tend to intimidate and lose the reader by virtue of their sheer size and volume of information. However, now that you have been introduced to written works about money and absorbed the information presented here, I certainly hope you will follow up by reading and studying some of the more comprehensive works available in libraries, bookstores and online. I gain nothing when you purchase and read someone else's financial book, but you do.

Appendix

Here you will find samples of an amortization chart and a checkbook register. Look them over.

A sample amortization chart. For a thirty year mortgage, it would be 360 lines long, but for illustrative purposes, I cut out the middle.

No.	Payment Date	Beginning Balance	Payment	Principal	Interest	Ending Balance
1	2/1/1985	$ 44,000.00	$ 521.34	$ 8.01	$ 513.33	$ 43,991.99
2	3/1/1985	$ 43,991.99	$ 521.34	$ 8.10	$ 513.24	$ 43,983.89
3	4/1/1985	$ 43,983.89	$ 521.34	$ 8.20	$ 513.15	$ 43,975.69
356	9/1/2014	$ 2,517.91	$ 521.34	$ 491.97	$ 29.38	$ 2,025.94
357	10/1/2014	$ 2,025.94	$ 521.34	$ 497.71	$ 23.64	$ 1,528.23
358	11/1/2014	$ 1,528.23	$ 521.34	$ 503.51	$ 17.83	$ 1,024.72
359	12/1/2014	$ 1,024.72	$ 521.34	$ 509.39	$ 11.96	$ 515.33
360	1/1/2015	$ 515.33	$ 521.34	$ 515.33	$ 6.01	$ (0.00)

This shows the first three and last five mortgage payments for a $44,000 house I bought in December

1985 at the ridiculously high interest rate of 14% (for 30 years), but the interest rate is not the focus here and neither is the price of the house. This is to show an example of an amortization table, and to illustrate how the lending institution gets their interest money up front.

Line No.1: Notice my first payment of $521.34. Only $8.01 goes toward paying down my house while a full $513.33 interest goes into the bank's pocket. The first three payments I made totaled $1,564.02, yet I only paid down my house by $24.31.

Lines 357-360: The last several payments show that eventually, more money from my $521.34 payment went toward the principal to actually pay off my house, than to the bank's coffers.

****

Following is a screenshot of a checkbook register.

Excuse the sloppy scribbling. You can see what was carried over from the previous page ($279.00), a deposit of ($150), and each check as the amount is written down and subtracted, revealing each and every time how much money is left. The register makes it difficult to accidentally spend more that you have.

NUMBER OR CODE	DATE	TRANSACTION DESCRIPTION	PAYMENT, FEE, WITHDRAWAL (-)	✓	DEPOSIT, CREDIT (+)	BALANCE $ 279.00
2857	11/19	Shoes from Mady's	23 49			− 23 49
						255 51
	11/21	Deposit			150 00	+ 150 00
						405 51
2588	11/21	Dinner at CRAB House	19 87			− 19 87
						385 64
2589	11/22	Electric Bill	223 17			− 223 17
						162 47
2590	11/23	Dollar Store	12 86			− 12 86
						149 61

AD - Automatic Deposit • AP - Automatic Payment • ATM - Cash Withdrawal • MD - Mobile Deposit • DC - Debit Card • FT - Funds Transfer • SC - Service Charge • TD - Tax Deductible

Here, I have $149.61 left in my account. As you can see, it's a simple task to keep track of your money. It's elementary school math, and you can do it!

Wishing you the best on all your money matters.